Game Changer
Playbook #3

UNSHAKEABLE
WORDS

90 Days of Fearless Declarations

TAMMY ADELE WILLIAMS

Printed in the United States of America

Cover Design by Adele

First Printing, 2025

ISBN: 978-0-9669254-7-0

Tammy'Dele Publishing

145 Robinson Drive

Fayetteville, Georgia 30214

www.TammyDelePublishing.com

This book belongs to

_____.

Date

_____

This book is lovingly dedicated to the unstoppable, determined spirit within us all.

SPECIAL THANKS

To all who played a role, big or small, in bringing this book to life, I appreciate you more than words can express. Thank you!

A heartfelt gratitude to the game changers in my life, Alvin Williams and Terence Johnson, my extended family, and a host of friends—my tribe. Thank you for always inspiring me to dream forward.

A very special thank you to my Mom, my greatest cheerleader, whose love and support continue to uplift me, even in her absence.✝ I am the hairdresser's daughter.

TABLE OF CONTENTS

"I am no longer accepting the things I cannot change.

I am changing the things I cannot accept."

Angela Davis

THE MOTIVATION

What do you really think about yourself -deep down inside? Do you need to level-up on your self-talk ?

What if I told you that you have the power to change your life—starting with your thoughts? The way you think about yourself, your future, and your purpose shapes the life you live. And here's the best part—you have the ability to take control of your mindset and step into something greater!

If you want to be a game changer—someone who not only transforms their own life but also inspires and impacts others—you have to start thinking like one. The most successful people, the biggest innovators, the greatest Olympians, and the greatest leaders all made a decision to think differently. They chose to believe in their potential, speak life over their circumstances, and take action with confidence. And guess what? You can do the same!

This book is your 90-day journey to a more powerful, joyful, and purpose-driven life. Each day, you'll speak positive, life-changing confessions that will help you build confidence, strengthen your faith, and push past any doubts or fears. Your words have power, and when you start declaring truth over your life, amazing things begin to happen.

Game changers don't wait for things to get better—they make things better by changing the way they think, speak, and act. You were created for greatness, and this is your time to step into it!

Get ready to unlock your potential, embrace a winning mindset, and walk boldly into the life you were meant to live. Let's go!

LET'S START WITH YOUR INTRODUCTION:

Hello.

My name is_____.

I'm a game changer.

I change game.

Any questions?

INSTRUCTIONS

Read one declaration per day.

Meditate on it and repeat until it becomes second nature.

Once it's second nature, check the box at the bottom of the page.

PART 1

I KNOW ME.

TRANSFORMING THE WAY I THINK ABOUT ME

WEEK 1

BUILDING YOUR BELIEVE SYSTEM

DAY 1

I wholeheartedly believe in myself, and I am worth every effort, every victory, and every breakthrough!

☐ GOT IT.

DAY 2

I am unstoppable. Challenges don't break me—they build me. Every obstacle is an opportunity, and I rise every time.

☐ GOT IT.

DAY 3

I own my greatness. I was born to create impact, to shift atmospheres, and to lead with purpose. Playing small is not an option.

☐ GOT IT.

DAY 4

I turn problems into power. No situation has control over me. I dictate my response, and I choose strength, wisdom, and resilience.

☐ GOT IT.

DAY 5

I am the answer. Where others see impossibility, I see innovation. I bring solutions, creativity, and vision everywhere.

☐ GOT IT.

DAY 6

I am built for greatness. Everything I need to succeed is already inside me.

☐ GOT IT.

DAY 7

I refuse to play small. I was born to make an impact, and I step into that truth daily.

☐ GOT IT.

WEEK 2

EMBRACING THE NOW

DAY 8

My past does not define me—my vision does. I am focused on the future I am creating.

☐ GOT IT.

DAY 9

I am worthy of success, happiness, and abundance. I don't just hope for great things—I expect them.

☐ GOT IT.

DAY 10

I show up as my highest self every day. I walk, talk, and think like the game changer I am.

☐ GOT IT.

DAY 11

I embrace my uniqueness. What makes
me different is what makes me
powerful.

☐ GOT IT.

DAY 12

I am a limitless being. There is no ceiling to what I can achieve.

☐ GOT IT.

DAY 13

I think like a champion, I act like a leader, and I win like a game changer!

☐ GOT IT.

DAY 14

I had a purpose before others had an opinion.

☐ GOT IT.

WEEK 3
BUILDING RESILIENCE & CONFIDENCE

DAY 15

I am not afraid of failure—it is simply a stepping stone to my next victory.

☐ GOT IT.

DAY 16

I am stronger than my struggles. No setback can keep me from my destiny.

☐ GOT IT.

DAY 17

I do not shrink in the face of challenges.
I rise, I learn, and I conquer.

☐ GOT IT.

DAY 18

I trust myself completely. My instincts, wisdom, and experience guide me toward success.

☐ GOT IT.

DAY 19

I walk into every room with confidence
because I know I belong there.

☐ GOT IT.

DAY 20

I release all self-doubt. I am qualified, capable, and ready to win.

☐ GOT IT.

DAY 21

I don't wait for permission to be great—I claim my greatness now.

☐ GOT IT.

WEEK 4
MINDSET & MENTAL
MASTERY

DAY 22

My mind is my most powerful asset. I train it daily for success.

☐ GOT IT.

DAY 23

I control my thoughts, and my thoughts create my reality. I think powerfully.

☐ GOT IT.

DAY 24

I don't let negativity take root in my mind. I choose faith over fear, hope over doubt.

☐ GOT IT.

DAY 25

I speak life over myself. My words shape my future, and I declare only good things.

☐ GOT IT.

DAY 26

I protect my energy. I do not entertain toxic thoughts, people, or situations.

☐ GOT IT.

DAY 27

I focus on progress, not perfection.
Every step forward is a victory.

☐ GOT IT.

DAY 28

I am not my mistakes. I grow, I improve,
and I become wiser every day.

☐ GOT IT.

WEEK 5
PURPOSE, PASSION & LEGACY

DAY 29

I wake up with purpose. My life has meaning, and I make every day count.

☐ GOT IT.

DAY 30

I am aligned with my calling. The work I do impacts lives in ways I can't even imagine.

☐ GOT IT.

DAY 31

I don't chase success—I attract it by becoming the best version of myself.

☐ GOT IT.

DAY 32

My dreams are valid, and I have everything I need to turn them into reality.

☐ GOT IT.

DAY 33

I am passionate about my journey. I embrace every lesson, every win, and every challenge.

☐ GOT IT.

DAY 34

I operate in excellence. Everything I touch turns to gold because I give my best effort.

☐ GOT IT.

DAY 35

I am creating a legacy. The impact I make today will be felt for generations.

☐ GOT IT.

WEEK 6
ABUNDANCE, JOY &
GRATITUDE

DAY 36

I am a magnet for success, joy, and abundance. Good things constantly flow into my life.

☐ GOT IT.

DAY 37

I wake up every day grateful. Gratitude shifts my mindset and multiplies my blessings.

☐ GOT IT.

DAY 38

I deserve happiness, and I don't need a reason to smile—I create my own joy.

☐ GOT IT.

DAY 39

I celebrate my wins, big and small.
Every step forward is worth
acknowledging.

☐ GOT IT.

DAY 40

I am surrounded by opportunities. I keep my eyes open and seize every one.

☐ GOT IT.

DAY 41

I love myself completely. I embrace my strengths, my flaws, and everything that makes me me.

☐ GOT IT.

DAY 42

I am a game changer, and the world is better because I show up as my best self every day!

☐ GOT IT.

WEEK 7
HONORING MY BODY

DAY 43

My body is my temple, and I treat it
with love, care, and respect.

☐ GOT IT.

DAY 44

I nourish myself with healthy food, movement, and rest because I deserve to feel strong and energized.

☐ GOT IT.

DAY 45

I listen to my body and honor what it needs—whether that's activity, stillness, or restoration.

☐ GOT IT.

DAY 46

Rest is productive. I allow myself to recharge without guilt.

☐ GOT IT.

DAY 47

I move my body with joy and appreciation, knowing that every step I take strengthens me.

☐ GOT IT.

DAY 48

I am patient with my body's journey.
Progress matters more than perfection.

☐ GOT IT.

DAY 49

I embrace my body as it is while working toward my healthiest self with love and gratitude.

☐ GOT IT.

WEEK 8

STRENGTHENING MY MIND

DAY 50

My mind is a powerhouse, and I fill it with thoughts that empower and uplift me.

☐ GOT IT.

DAY 51

I guard my mental space. I release stress, worry, and negativity that do not serve me.

☐ GOT IT.

DAY 52

I am committed to lifelong learning.
Every day is an opportunity to grow in
wisdom and knowledge.

☐ GOT IT.

DAY 53

I practice mindfulness and presence. I refuse to let my thoughts dwell on the past or the future—I choose now.

☐ GOT IT.

DAY 54

I silence self-doubt with self-belief. My thoughts are my greatest allies, not my enemies.

☐ GOT IT.

DAY 55

I take breaks when needed. Mental clarity is just as important as productivity.

☐ GOT IT.

DAY 56

I speak kindly to myself. My words shape my reality, and I choose words that build me up.

☐ GOT IT.

WEEK 9

NURTURING MY SPIRIT

DAY 57

My spirit is powerful, and I feed it daily
with peace, love, and faith.

☐ GOT IT.

DAY 58

I create space for stillness. In quiet
moments, I find clarity, wisdom, and
divine guidance.

☐ GOT IT.

DAY 59

I let go of what I cannot control.
Surrendering brings peace, not
weakness.

☐ GOT IT.

DAY 60

I cultivate inner joy that is not
dependent on circumstances. My
happiness comes from within.

☐ GOT IT.

DAY 61

I am deeply connected to my purpose.
Every action I take aligns with the
mission I am here to fulfill.

☐ GOT IT.

DAY 62

I trust the process. Everything is
unfolding for my highest good, even
when I don't see it yet.

☐ GOT IT.

DAY 63

My faith is stronger than my fears. I walk boldly, knowing that I am guided and supported.

☐ GOT IT.

WEEK 10

MASTERING MY EMOTIONS

DAY 64

I honor my emotions without letting them control me. I feel, process, and release with wisdom.

☐ GOT IT.

DAY 65

I create emotional boundaries that protect my peace. Not everything deserves my energy.

☐ GOT IT.

DAY 66

I give myself permission to heal. I am not my past, and I am free to move forward.

☐ GOT IT.

DAY 67

I choose to respond, not react. My emotions do not dictate my decisions—wisdom does.

☐ GOT IT.

DAY 68

I cultivate relationships that bring me joy, support, and growth. I let go of what drains me.

☐ GOT IT.

DAY 69

I allow myself to feel deeply, knowing that vulnerability is a strength, not a weakness.

☐ GOT IT.

DAY 70

I am in control of my inner world. No external situation can shake my peace.

☐ GOT IT.

WEEK 11
TOTAL SELF-CARE
ALIGNMENT

DAY 71

I am a priority in my own life. Taking care of myself allows me to give my best to the world.

☐ GOT IT.

DAY 72

My self-care is non-negotiable. I invest in myself because I am worth it.

☐ GOT IT.

DAY 73

I create balance in my life. I make time for work, rest, love, and play.

☐ GOT IT.

DAY 74

I protect my peace at all costs. No one else is responsible for my well-being but me.

☐ GOT IT.

DAY 75

I lead by example. When I take care of myself, I inspire others to do the same.

☐ GOT IT.

DAY 76

I fill my own cup first, knowing that I serve others best when I am whole.

☐ GOT IT.

DAY 77

I am committed to my body, mind, spirit, and emotions. When I am well, I am unstoppable!

☐ GOT IT.

PART 2

I SEE YOU.

TRANSFORMING THE WAY I SEE OTHERS

WEEK 12

SEEING THE BEST IN OTHERS

DAY 78

I see the greatness in others, and I call it out. I am surrounded by world-changers, and I choose to uplift them.

☐ GOT IT.

DAY 79

I celebrate others without comparison. Their success does not diminish mine—it inspires me to go higher.

☐ GOT IT.

DAY 80

I give people grace because I know everyone is on a journey. I choose understanding over judgment.

☐ GOT IT.

DAY 81

I believe in others even when they don't believe in themselves. My encouragement has the power to awaken purpose.

☐ GOT IT.

DAY 82

I treat people with kindness, knowing that even the smallest act of love can change a life.

☐ GOT IT.

DAY 83

I recognize the potential in every person I meet. No one is ordinary— everyone carries something valuable.

☐ GOT IT.

DAY 84

I am intentional about building people up. I use my words to inspire, not to tear down.

☐ GOT IT.

WEEK 13
COLLABORATION OVER COMPETITION

DAY 85

I don't compete—I collaborate. There is more than enough room for everyone to win.

☐ GOT IT.

DAY 86

I connect with others with an open heart, knowing that strong relationships create strong opportunities.

☐ GOT IT.

DAY 87

I attract high-caliber people because I give high-caliber energy. I bring value wherever I go.

☐ GOT IT.

DAY 88

I listen with the intent to understand, not just to respond. This makes me a powerful communicator.

☐ GOT IT.

DAY 89

I respect different perspectives. Growth comes when I am open to learning from others.

☐ GOT IT.

DAY 90

I embrace teamwork because I know that together, we achieve more than we ever could alone.

☐ GOT IT.

BEYOND
90 DAYS BONUS

WEEK 14
LEADERSHIP & INFLUENCE

DAY 91

I am not intimidated by others'
success—I celebrate it because success
is contagious.

☐ GOT IT.

DAY 92

I lead with integrity, knowing that my actions set the tone for those around me.

☐ GOT IT.

DAY 93

I treat everyone with respect. It's the human being over the title. Every person deserves honor.

☐ GOT IT.

DAY 94

I am a leader who lifts others higher. My influence is a force for good in the world.

☐ GOT IT.

DAY 95

I recognize that leadership is service. The more I help others, the greater my impact becomes.

☐ GOT IT.

DAY 96

I invest in people, knowing that mentorship and encouragement create lasting change.

☐ GOT IT.

DAY 97

I surround myself with dreamers and doers. Iron sharpens iron, and I thrive in an environment of excellence.

☐ GOT IT.

DAY 98

I empower others by being authentic.
My transparency gives others
permission to be real too.

☐ GOT IT.

WEEK 15
LOVE, LEGACY & PURPOSE

DAY 99

I see people beyond their past. I believe in redemption, growth, and second chances.

☐ GOT IT.

DAY 100

I create a legacy of love, knowing that how I treat people will outlive me.

☐ GOT IT.

DAY 101

I love without limits. My ability to care
for others is a reflection of my strength,
not my weakness.

☐ GOT IT.

DAY 102

I refuse to let bitterness block my blessings. Forgiveness frees me to move forward.

☐ GOT IT.

DAY 103

I attract positive relationships because I radiate trust, loyalty, and kindness.

☐ GOT IT.

DAY 104

I see divine connections in every interaction. No meeting is by accident— every person I encounter has purpose.

☐ GOT IT.

DAY 105

I am a vessel of encouragement. My words, actions, and presence inspire others to believe in themselves.

☐ GOT IT.

DAY 106

I am a game changer, and part of my mission is to help others win. When they rise, I rise too.

☐ GOT IT.

DAY 107

I love people well because at the end of the day, success isn't just about what I accomplish—it's about the lives I touch.

☐ GOT IT.

FINAL THOUGHTS

As you continue to move forward in your journey, remember this, **you are your greatest asset.** Care for yourself with the same energy you give to your goals, because your well-being is the foundation of your success. You are a game changer. The way you think, speak, and act has the power to shape the world around you. **Never underestimate the impact of your presence.**

Tomorrow's uncertainties can be the catalyst for fear and anxiety, allowing the negative "what ifs" to bombard your mind. Know there is something powerful about the energy you carry. Refuse to give problems power over you. When circumstances absolutely can't be changed, shift your perspective— because your mindset is your superpower. Stay focused. Stay strong, and stay positively charged.

Nothing can stop you from moving forward. You are built to win. Now go, step boldly into the greatness that is already yours and change game!

ABOUT

TAMMY ADELE WILLIAMS

Tammy Williams is the inspiring CEO of Tammy'Dele Films and a proud co-owner of CS-145 Studios. In 2012, she made history as the first African American woman to own and operate a studio and post-production facility in Georgia, breaking new ground in the industry.

With over 30 years in the broadcast world, Williams started her journey as an editor at WTVF (CBS) in Nashville, TN. Her career has blossomed into a diverse portfolio filled with writing, directing, and producing films, television shows, biographies, documentaries, and network news. She also brings a wealth of experience in live award show creative direction, writing, and producing.

In addition to her work in film and television, Williams is an accomplished author and motivational speaker, sharing her experiences and insights to inspire others.

Williams is passionate about empowering women of color through her creation of Naturally Brown Woman. Naturally Brown Woman is an educational collective, that focuses on helping women by sharing valuable resources, ideas, and concepts.

Furthermore, Williams founded Tammy'Dele Films Workshops, which offers workshops and job training.

She is also a proud graduate of Middle Tennessee State University, where she earned her B.S. in Mass Communications, focusing on Radio/Television Production. She is a member of Alpha Kappa Alpha Sorority, Inc.

Together with her husband, the talented industry mogul Alvin Williams, she continues to build their dreams both at home and in their exciting business ventures.

132